ANCIENT CIVILIZATIONS OF ISLAM

Muslim History for Kids
Early Dynasties

Ancient History for Kids

6th Grade Social Studies

Speedy Publishing LLC
40 E. Main St. #1156
Newark, DE 19711
www.speedypublishing.com

In this book, we're going to talk about the ancient civilizations of Islam. So, let's get right to it!

During the Middle Ages, while the culture of Europe declined, the empire of Islam was expanding in the countries of the Middle East. Over 28% of the world's population was part of the Islamic Empire at its peak. It grew to become a prosperous and advanced culture.

VILLAGE LIFE OF BAALBEK, LEBANON

HOLY QURAN

WHEN DID THE ISLAMIC RELIGION AND THE ISLAMIC EMPIRE BEGIN?

The prophet Muhammad established Islam in 610 CE. A person who believes in the Islamic religion is called a Muslim. Just as Christians read and study the Bible as their guidebook, Muslims read and study their holy book, which is entitled the Quran.

They declare that the words of the Quran were given to Muhammad through Gabriel, the archangel. They believe that the words were from Allah, their one true god.

QURAN

THE FIVE PILLAR OF ISLAM

THE FIVE TENETS OF ISLAM

There are five basic principles that Muslims live by. They are:

Shahadah

The Shahadah is the statement of faith that Muslims pray at each session. In that statement, they declare the one true god and affirm that Muhammad was Allah's messenger.

Salat or Prayer

The Salat are the five prayer sessions that Muslims make daily. They must turn their bodies and faces to the sacred city of Mecca when they recite their prayers.

They kneel down on a prayer mat and use some repetitive motions such as bowing and touching their foreheads to the ground when they pray.

MUSLIMS GATHERED IN MECCA OF THE WORLD'S DIFFERENT COUNTRIES

Happy
Eid Mubarak
ZAKAT

Zakat

The Zakat is the action of providing for those who cannot take care of themselves. The Muslims who can afford to do so are strongly encouraged to give their money to those who are needy.

MUSLIM WOMAN FASTING PRAY TO ALLAH OVER SUNSET

Fasting

During Ramadan, the month of fasting, Muslims follow a practice of fasting from the time the sun rises to when the sun sets. They believe that fasting brings them into alignment with Allah.

Hajj

All Muslims are strongly encouraged to make the trip to Mecca during their lifetimes. This special journey is called the hajj.

THE SPREAD OF ISLAM

At the beginning, the prophet Muhammad encountered resistance to his holy message. However, over time, he had many followers. The religion of Islam also became the form of government as it spread from the city of Mecca, located in the country known as Saudi Arabia today, to the region of the Middle East.

A MOSQUE

SHEIKH ZAYED MOSQUE, GRAND MOSQUE, ABU DHABI

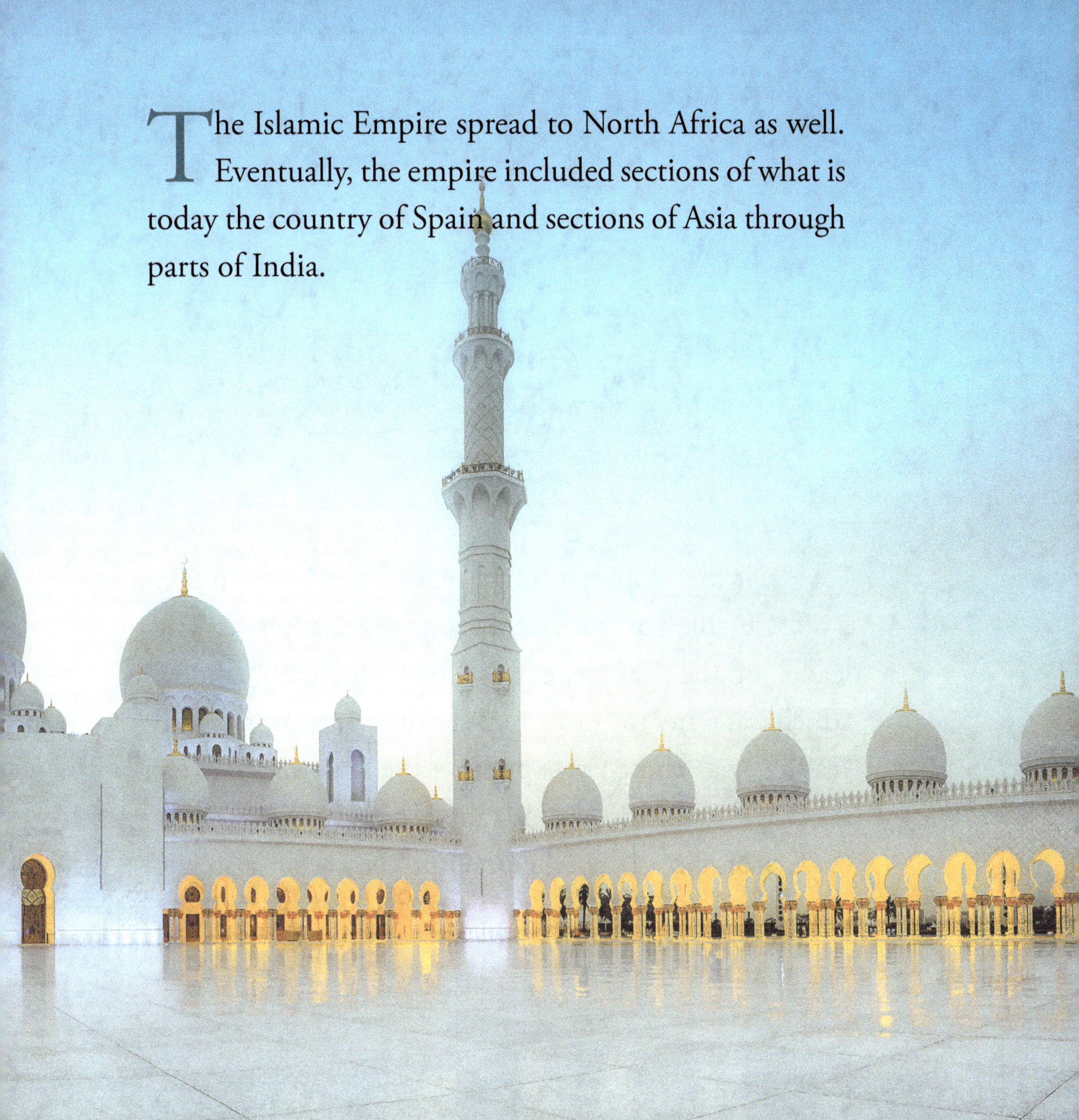

The Islamic Empire spread to North Africa as well. Eventually, the empire included sections of what is today the country of Spain and sections of Asia through parts of India.

THE CALIPHATE

After the prophet Muhammad passed away in 632 CE, the government became the Caliphate. The leader of the Caliphate was known as the "caliph," which translates to "successor." The reason that the word "caliph" was chosen was because the first leaders were related to Muhammad. The caliphs became the religious leaders of the Islam religion, but they were also the governmental leaders.

ALI BEN-HAMET
CALIPH OF CONSTANTINE AND
CHIEF OF THE HARACTAS

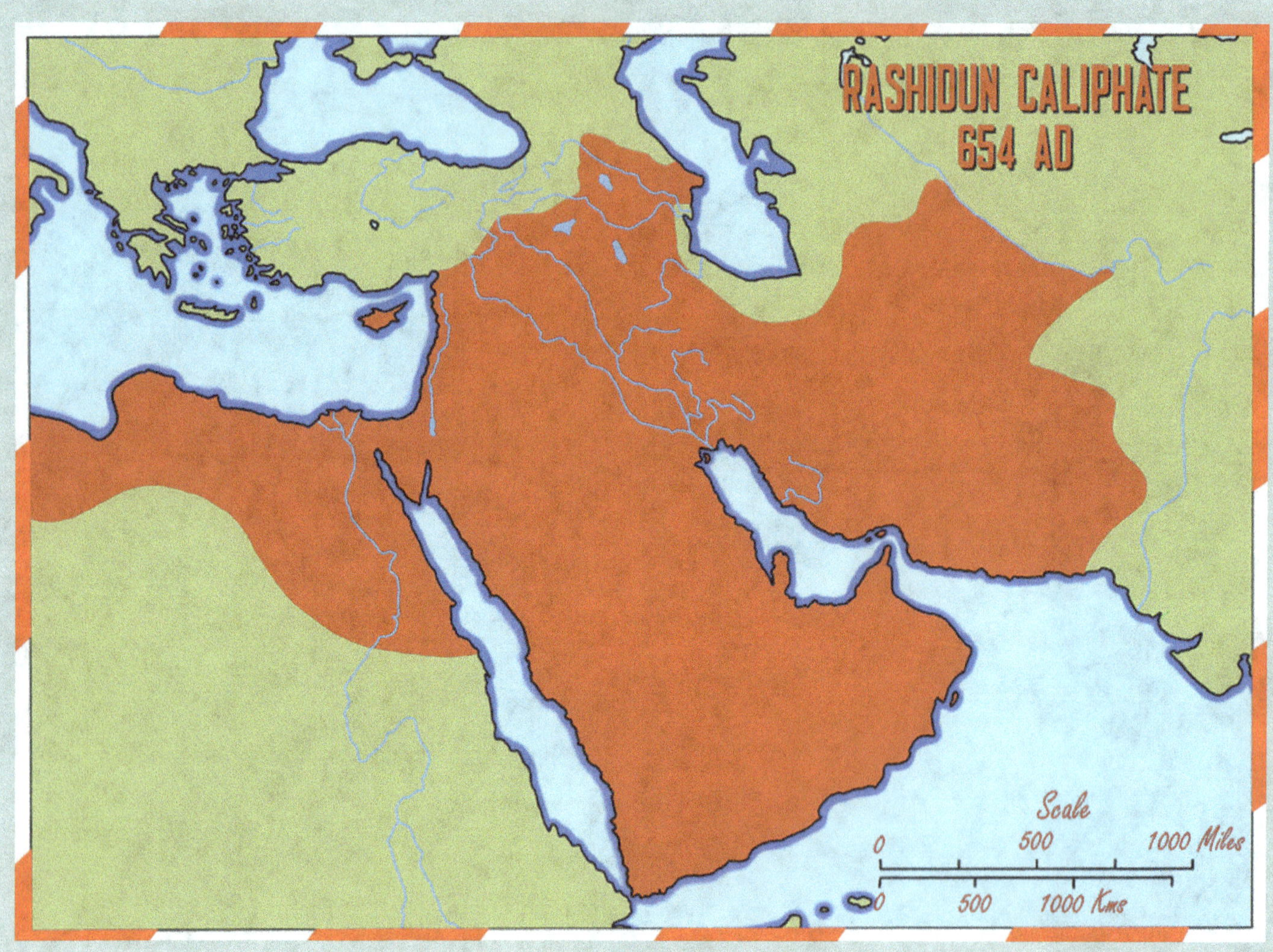

ORIGINAL HAND DRAWN MAP. THE RASHIDUN CALIPHATE IN 654 AD

THE FIRST CALIPHATE—RASHIDUN

The first four caliphs of the empire learned about Islam directly from the prophet Muhammad. Because of this, Muslims call them the "rightly guided" caliphs.

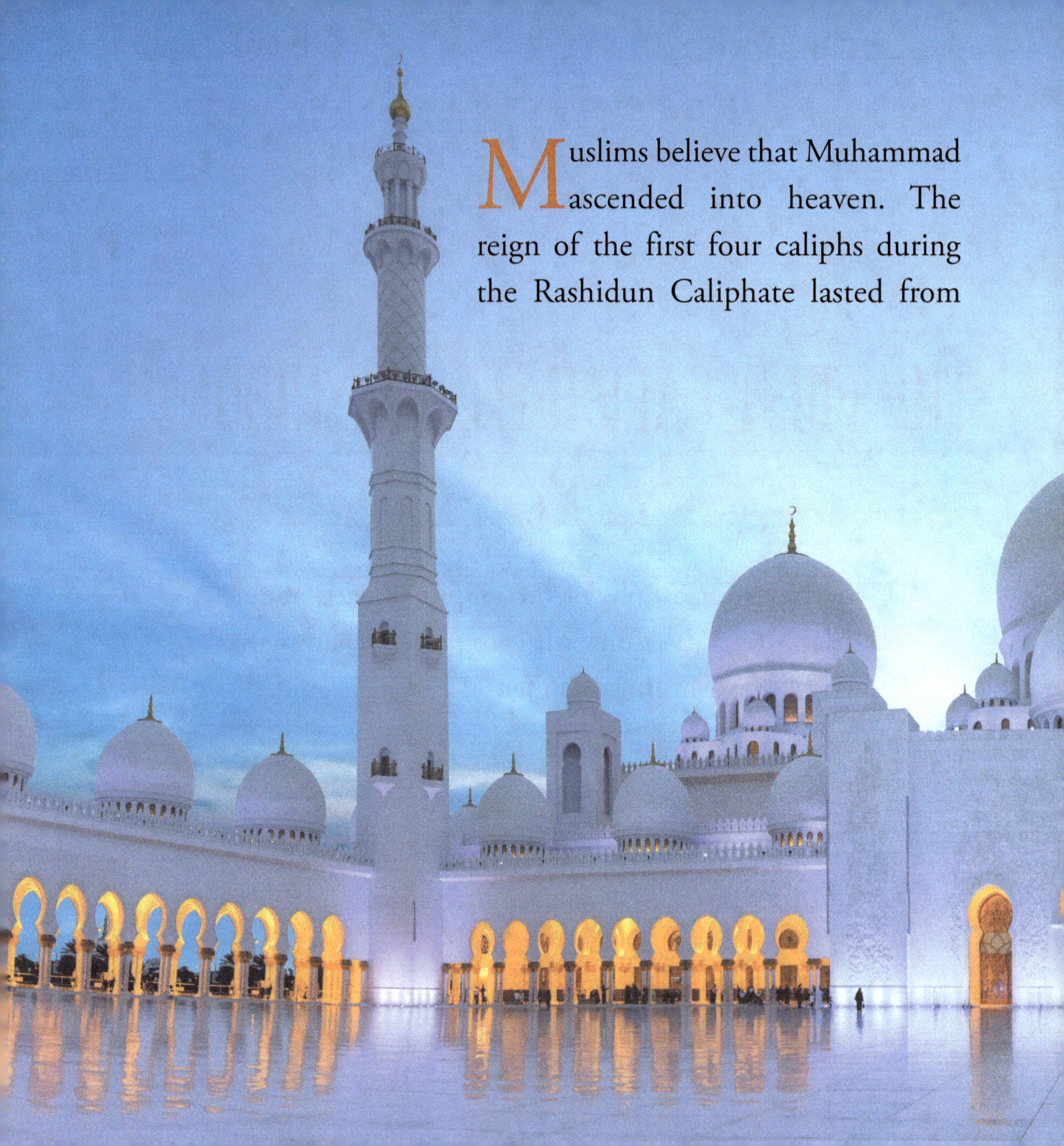

Muslims believe that Muhammad ascended into heaven. The reign of the first four caliphs during the Rashidun Caliphate lasted from

632 CE, when Muhammad passed away, to the year 661 CE, almost 30 years. The city of Medina was the first capital city of the empire.

MUSLIM PILGRIMS AT THE KAABA IN THE GREAT MOSQUE OF MECCA, SAUDI ARABIA, DURING HAJJ

Abu Bakr, the first caliph

Abu Bakr ruled the empire for two years from 632 to 634 CE. He was the father of one of Muhammad's wives. He had quickly converted to Islam. His major achievement was to squelch the uprising from non-Muslim rebels from Arabic tribes. He was successful in his efforts to establish and stabilize the Caliphate. He was also the first leader of the original hajj to the city of Mecca.

Umar ibn (son of) al-Khattab, the second caliph

In Muslim names, the word "ibn" means "son of." At the beginning, Umar was against Muhammad and wanted

MUSLIM MAN AND WOMAN PRAYING IN MOSQUE

to assassinate him. However, he was converted when his best friend and family members became Muslims. He became a close follower of Muhammad.

MUSLIM WOMAN READING BOOK

IEW OF THE MOSQUES OF SULTAN
HASSAN AND AL-RIFAI IN CAIRO

After Muhammad and the first caliph passed away, Umar ruled for a decade, from 634 to 644 CE. He added lands to the empire as he brought regions of Egypt as well as Syria and North Africa under Islamic rule. He was admired as a strong, pious leader who could discern between right action and wrong action. He was also a powerful athlete. His reign came to an end when he was killed by a slave from Persia.

Uthman ibn (son of) Affan, the third caliph

Like Abu, Uthman was related to the prophet. He married one of Muhammad's daughters and when she passed away, he married one of her sisters. He reigned from 644 to 656 CE. One of his major achievements was that he established an official copy of the holy book, the Quran. The original version had been assembled by Abu Bakr. From then on, Uthman's version was considered the final version. His reign ended when he was murdered by anti-Muslim rebels.

HOLY QURAN

GRAND MOSQUE OF KUFA

Ali ibn (son of) Abi Talib, the fourth caliph

Ali was Muhammad's son-in-law and also his cousin. Ali was the husband of Fatimah, who was the prophet's youngest daughter. Ali was the ruler from 656 to 661 CE. He was admired as a wise and holy leader who was masterful at speeches as well as proverbs. His reign came to an end when he was murdered during a prayer session at the city of Kufa's Great Mosque.

THE SECOND CALIPHATE—UMAYYAD

The next Caliphate after the Rashidun Caliphate was the Umayyad Caliphate, which was an Islamic dynasty. The definition of a dynasty is that the empire's rule was hereditary and passed from father to son. If the ruler didn't have an heir, he might pass the rule to another male relative.

MUAWIYAH PALACE AND MOSQUE OF IMAM ALI IN KUFA NEAR NAJAF, IRAQ

UMAYYAD MOSQUE IN ANCIENT CITY OF DAMASCUS (SYRIAN ARAB REPUBLIC)

The Umayyads ruled from 661 to 750 CE, almost 90 years. After the Civil War that took place, Muawiyah I took power and became Caliph.

He moved the capital city to Damascus. The Umayyads ruled from there until 750 CE when the Abbasid Caliphate overthrew them.

ABBASID CALIPHATE FORTRESS

CONTRIBUTIONS OF THE UMAYYADS

The Umayyads did much to make the Islamic Empire stronger. Here are some of their contributions and achievements.

They expanded the empire to include more of northern Africa, the Iberian Peninsula, and more of the Middle East into Asia and India. At their height, over 60 million people were under their rule, almost one-third of the world's inhabitants.

UMAYYAD MOSQUE

They structured their government after the government of the Byzantines. The Byzantine government had ruled much of the land that the Umayyads had conquered and brought into the Islamic Empire.

THE SEIZURE OF EDESSA IN SYRIA BY THE BYZANTINE ARMY

The Umayyads appointed governors to run smaller regions described as provinces. They also created "diwans," which were governing bodies to handle the needed administrative work of the regional government agencies.

Because there were so many different cultures that were now part of their empire, the Umayyads felt it was important to unify them. They created standard coins, a standard language, which was Arabic, and they also standardized measurements. These commonalities helped to unify the different people within the realm.

A TYPICAL ARAB FAMILY

They were avid builders and created a number of architecturally amazing mosques worldwide, such as the important mosque in Jerusalem, which is called the **Dome of the Rock**.

DOME OF THE ROCK

GREAT MOSQUE OF UMMAYADS

Toward the end of their reign, the Umayyads were criticized for venturing too far away from Islamic ideals.

In 750 CE, an opposing group described as the Abbasids came to power and took over. They would rule for the next few centuries.

MONGOL WARRIORS

THE THIRD CALIPHATE-ABBASID

The Abbasids ruled over two distinct periods of time. From 750 to 1258 CE, they had a solid hold over the empire. This was the time that historians describe as the "Golden Age" of Islam. However, in 1258, Baghdad, which was the capital at the time, was looted and destroyed by the Mongols. The Abbasids escaped to the city of Cairo in Egypt. They retained their religious leadership, which they continued through 1517 CE, but not their political leadership.

CONTRIBUTIONS OF THE ABBASIDS

The Abbasids ruled for many centuries. Their early rule was characterized by peace as well as prosperity. Here are some of their contributions and achievements during Islam's Golden Age, which took place from 790 to 1258 CE.

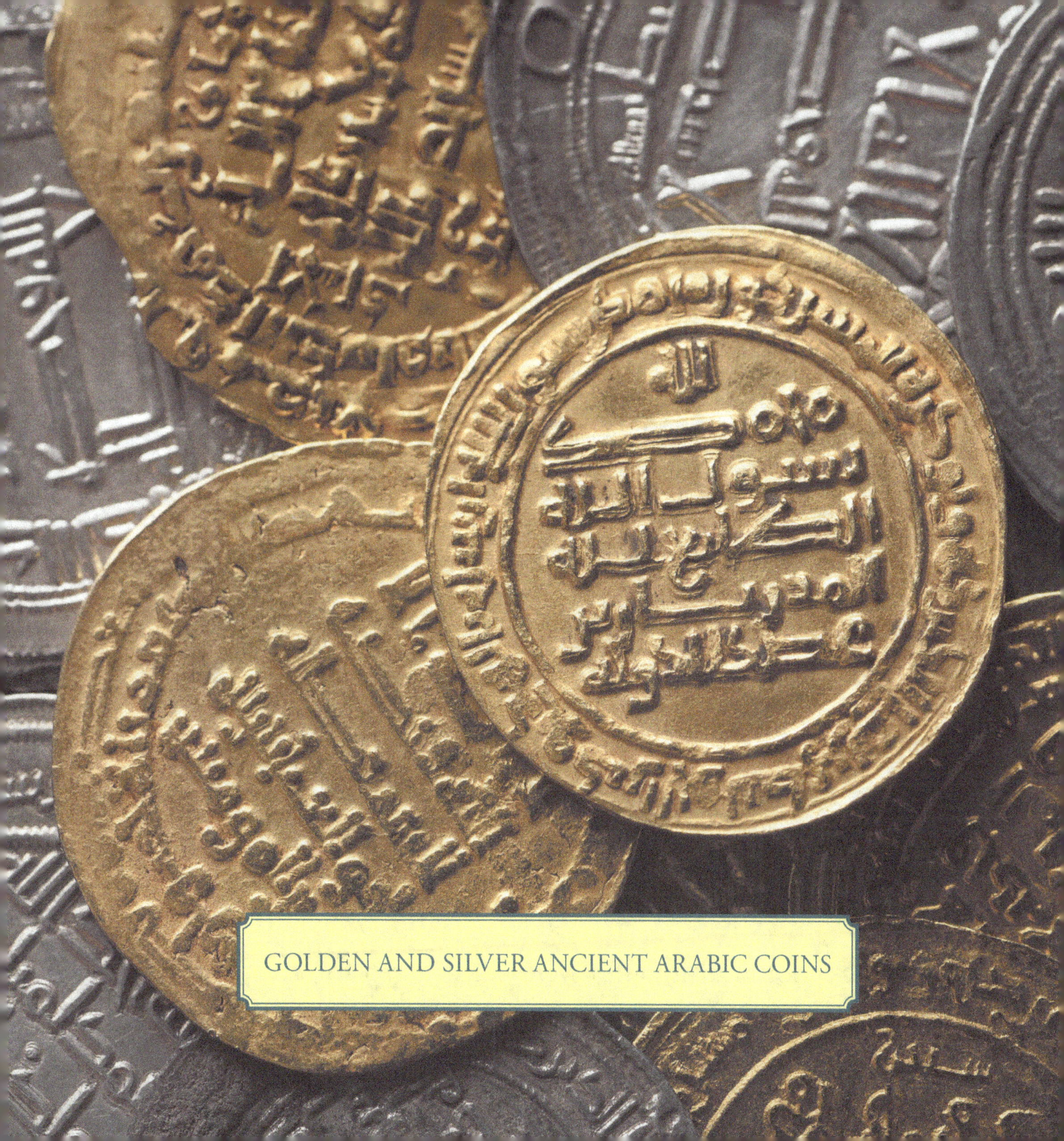

GOLDEN AND SILVER ANCIENT ARABIC COINS

During this period, there were huge advances in science as well as in mathematics.

- Schools and libraries were constructed to meet the demands throughout the empire.

- Innovations in medical practices were happening at a rapid pace.
- Architecture was flourishing and so was art.
- Scholars from all over the world came to Baghdad to debate and translate the classic works into different languages.

MOSQUE OF IBN TULUN

SUMMARY

The prophet Muhammad established the Islamic religion in 610 CE. At the beginning, he was persecuted, but eventually he gained many followers. After Muhammad passed away, the Caliphate was established. The first Caliphate was the Rashidun Caliphate, which lasted for almost 30 years. The next Caliphate was the Umayyad Caliphate, which lasted for almost 90 years followed by the Abbasid Caliphate.

Now that you've read about the ancient civilizations of Islam, you may want to read about the scientists and scholars of the early Islamic world in the Baby Professor book Scientists and Scholars of the Early Islamic World - Islamic Empire History Book 3rd Grade | Children's History.

Visit
BABY PROFESSOR
EDUCATION KIDS
www.BabyProfessorBooks.com
to download Free Baby Professor eBooks
and view our catalog of new and exciting
Children's Books

www.ingramcontent.com/pod-product-compliance
Lightning Source LLC
LaVergne TN
LVHW060505170826
845677LV00026B/1627

* 9 7 9 8 8 6 9 4 3 7 3 2 7 *